Dear God

Nydia Hadi

BookLeaf Publishing

Presentation by *BookLeaf Publishing*

Web: www.bookleafpub.com

E-mail: info@bookleafpub.com

ISBN: 9789395756631

First edition 2022

Morning Prayer

Dear God,

Thank You for a new day.
I am excited to start my day today.
Please guard my thoughts, so that they will be
filled with positive thoughts.
Please guard my words, so that they will only
say positive words.
Please guard my doings, so that I behave godly
and holy.
Let me be a blessing to others today.
Thank You, God.

Amen

Night Prayer

Dear God,

Thank You for today.
I feel Your presence and guidance throughout
my day today.
Thank You for making me a better person day by
day.
Please forgive me if I hurt You or others today
by any chance.
I hope tomorrow will be better.
Thank You, God.

Amen

Prayer When In A Relationship

Dear God,

Thank You for answering my prayer and sending
(…) into my life.
I believe that You let us enter into each other's
life for good reasons.
Please guide us so that we can give each other
happiness, support, and love.
We want to love each other the way You love us.

Let us take care of each other;
Let us be a blessing in each other's life;
Let us inspire each other;
Let us become more selfless and love each other
unconditionally;
Let us appreciate each other;
Let us forgive each other and accept each other's
weaknesses;
Let us be grateful for each other's presence and
kindness instead of taking them for granted;
Let us become the best version of ourselves for
each other;
Let both of us be closer to You.

I invite You to always be present in our
relationship.
Only with Your presence and guidance that we
can fill this relationship with love, joy, peace,
and wisdom.
Thank You for this wonderful relationship, God.

Amen

Prayer When We Are Single

Dear God,

I know that being single is probably the best for me right now.
I may be happier being single than in a relationship at this moment.
I may not be ready for a relationship.
You may want me to learn something else first before entering into a relationship.
I know that I should be patient in waiting for Your plan to be revealed.

But if I can tell You the truth, God, sometimes I feel happy by myself.
But sometimes, I feel like nobody loves me or cares about me.
Or that I am not worthy of love.
Please help me overcome this loneliness, God.
The future seems very uncertain and scary without someone to share with.
Although I know that with You, I can feel complete and I do not have to be scared.
I know that You know what is best for me.

Please give me the patience and courage to live
my life right now.
Although I have no one by my side, I still have
many things to be grateful for.
If someday the right person comes into my life,
please help me be ready.
In the meantime, I will wait patiently and never
lose hope in You.
Thank You, God.

Amen

Prayer For Family

Dear God,

Thank You for giving me my family.
I cherish the moments when we share the love
and joy with each other.
Every smile, laughter, togetherness, support, and
comfort from my family is priceless.
When the world seems to be against me, I can
always turn to my family.

However, there were moments when we were
hurting each other.
It was very disappointing and painful.
Even when strangers hurt us, it was painful. Let
alone family.
Please help us reflect on our own faults and
weaknesses.
Please help us forgive each other and accept
each other's weaknesses.
Please give us the courage to apologize.
Please give us peace.

Hopefully we can learn something from any
conflicts and come out stronger as a family.

No matter what happened, I will always love my
family.
I always want them to be healthy and happy.

So, God, please protect my family.
Please let my presence be a blessing to them.
Please help me be more selfless so that I can
serve them more.
We never know how much time we can still
spend together.
Therefore, God, please never let me take them
for granted.

Amen

Prayer For Friends

Dear God,

I would like to thank You for sending good
friends to my life.
I am happy that there are people who care about
me like my friends.
I am also happy that I can care for them too.
Just being able to talk to them, to joke around, to
tell my problems, and to express my feelings,
make me feel good.
This social support in my life is very precious.

However, there were times when I did not feel
reciprocated by my friends.
There were times when I felt excluded.
There were times when I did not feel supported
or understood.

I tell myself, it is okay.
Nobody is perfect.
I am probably not a perfect friend, myself.

God, help me be more selfless, understanding,
and tolerant.

Guide me in my friendship so that I consider not only what they can do for me but also what I can do for them.
Help me see the world not only from my lenses but also from other people's lenses.
Help me communicate my feelings better so that there is no resentment built over time.

God, please protect my friends and give them happiness.
Thank You, God.

Amen

Gratitude Prayer

Dear God,

For every little thing in my life, such as:
Waking up in the morning,
being greeted by sunshine,
breathing fresh air,
the roof above my head,
the clothes I wear,
the food I eat,
doing activities,
spending time with the people I love,
and falling asleep,
I thank You, God.

Sometimes, we do not realize how privileges
these things are.
It is easy to get distracted by the busyness in
every day's life.
I do not want to take these blessings for granted.

For all the achievements and milestones that I
have accomplished, I also would like to thank
You, God.
I cannot do them without You.
I know that all of them are coming from You.

I have no rights to be prideful.
I want to give all the credits to You.

Sometimes I find myself enjoying city views
like the skyscrapers, houses, bridges, highways,
cars, and night lights.
Sometimes I find myself enjoying nature views
like ocean, lakes, mountains, forest, and blue
sky.
Wherever I am, I can see the beauty of creations.
Often, I find myself surrounded by people who
give me so much happiness and joy in my life.
They have touched my heart and made me feel
loved.
What have I done to deserve this beautiful life,
God?

If there is anything I can do for You, please let
me know.
Thank You, God, for everything.

Amen

Prayer For Work

Dear God,

I am grateful for the work opportunity that You gave me.
It helps me support myself.

There are days when I feel motivated and productive.
But there are days when I feel burned out.
There are days when I feel confident about my work.
But there are days when I doubt myself.
There are days when I get along well with my colleagues.
But there are days when we do not get along.
There are days when I feel secure.
But there are days when I feel competitive and insecure.

God, please guide me throughout these high and low phases at work.
Please give me the energy and the motivation that I need.

Please remind me to be grateful and to keep
doing what I am doing when things go well.
But please remind me to be patient, perseverant,
and to rely and trust You more when things do
not go well.
I believe that Your timing is always better than
my timing.
I believe that everything will come at the right
time.

Please help me focus on contributing to the
society instead of just focus on my own selfish
gain.
Please help me to stay humble whenever I
achieve something great.
Please take care of me, God.

Amen

Prayer For Anxiety

Dear God,

Although I keep reaching out to You, why do I still feel anxious?
I sometimes feel anxious about my job, my family, my future, my relationship, etc.
I am afraid that something will not go according to my plan.
I am afraid of failure and suffering.

I want to have more faith in You, God .
Regardless of what might happen, I know that Your plan is always better than my plan.
Whenever I hope for something, I will just hope that my plan aligns with Your plan.
But if not, please give me the courage to accept Your plan.

I realize that sometimes You take away things from me just to give me something better later on.
Sometimes You teach me life lessons that make me grow more mature, tougher, and wiser.

If I know that You love me and care for me, I
don't have to worry about life, don't I?
I will just focus on doing my best on the things
that I can control.
For the things in life that I cannot control, I will
entrust them to You, God.

Please continue to watch over me and take care
of me.
Please give me a peace of mind.
I would really appreciate it.

Thank You, God.

Amen

Prayer During Failure

Dear God,

I have just experienced a (or another) failure in
my life.
This is not what I expected.
Disappointment, embarrassment, low
self-esteem, all come together during this time.
All the effort that I have put in was apparently
not enough.
It is extremely hard to accept.
What could I have done differently?
Right now I cannot think of anything.
I don't like these painful and hopeless feelings.

I am glad that I have You, God.
Regardless of this failure, I know that I am
always good enough for You.
I don't have to achieve certain things to be
accepted by You.
I am still a worthy human being.

Maybe this failure is to prepare me to face even
bigger challenges in the future.
Maybe this failure teaches me to remain humble.
Maybe You have different plans for me.

Maybe in a few weeks or in a few months or
even in a few years, I would see this failure with
a grateful heart.
I know that I will learn something.
I know that this experience will push me to be
better.

But right now, please give me comfort, God.
Please ease my pain and my disappointment.
Please help me bounce back from this failure.
Please give me hope.

Thank You, God.

Amen

Prayer During Sickness

Dear God,

Sometimes, we don't realize how precious our
health is until we fall sick.
Maybe this is a reminder for me that in life, I am
not invincible.
I still need Your grace and protection.
Maybe this is a reminder for me to appreciate
my health more and take care of my body more.
I also would like to thank You for sending the
people who are taking care of me when I am
sick.

God, this feels very uncomfortable.
I hope You can heal me soon.
But I know that You never leave me alone.
When I suffer, You suffer with me too.

Thank You for always being with me.
Please don't let me lose hope in You.

Amen

Prayer When Experiencing Injustice

Dear God,

I don't know what I have done to receive this
unjust treatment.
I am very hurt and bitter by how they treated me.
Why did they do that to me?
Aren't I also a human being who has rights, just
like them?

God, please give me the strength and the
patience to forgive them.
It is hard, but it is not impossible with Your
grace.
It is easy to think about revenge.
But I know that I have no rights for revenge,
because they are also Your creations.
Maybe in the past, I did injustice to others too
that I did not realize.
I hope there will be reconciliation someday.

I don't want to be a victim anymore, God.
Please raise me up and make me tougher
regardless of the injustice that I experienced.
However, I cannot do this alone.

Please help me feel at peace.
Please be with me always and console me.

Thank You, God.

Amen

Prayer During Divorce or Break Up

Dear God,

Suddenly, the closest person to me is no longer there.
I feel very devastated.
Although there were a lot of arguments, conflicts, and resentment for a while, it is still disappointing knowing that it did not work between us.
I wish things could turn out differently.
I wish we were as compatible as before.

Now I am hopeless.
I have to get used to this new change in my life.
I used to picture my future with this person.
But now this image is shattered.
I have to face the world once again alone.

God, please help me forgive him/her and forgive myself.
I feel guilty for not being able to accept his/her shortcomings.
I know that I have a lot of shortcomings too.

Still, I have learned a lot from this relationship.
Maybe this person is not meant to be for me.
Maybe this experience will prepare me for the
next relationship.
I hope I can grow stronger, wiser, and more
mature.

Please forgive me, God, for not being strong or
wise enough in this relationship.
Please take away the pain from me.
Or at least bear it together with me so that I
don't feel alone anymore.

Thank You, God.

Amen

Prayer When Losing A Loved One

Dear God,

I have just lost my (…)
It is the worst feeling I have ever experienced.
Why did You take him/her from my life, God?
Now that he/she is gone, I feel so lost.
I used to rely on him/her a lot.
Now what am I supposed to do?
Whenever I remember the moments we have
spent together, I feel sad.
I keep remembering what he/she had said or
done to me.
Especially all the encouraging words,
consolation, support, and love.
I hope I will understand Your plan someday.

Maybe You took him/her because he/she
suffered a lot.
Maybe he/she will be much happier up there.
Maybe it's time for me to realize that I can only
rely on You.

God, please help me feel better again.

Please help me interpret this situation from Your
perspective and not from my own self-interest.
Please heal my wound.
Please take care of my (…).
I will be more at peace knowing that he/she is
with You forever in eternal life, where there is
no more suffering.
Instead, there will be joy and peace.

Thank You, God.

Amen

Prayer For Those Who Are Poor

Dear God,

Today I wanted to pray for those who are poor, especially those whose basic needs are not met. Please give shelter to the homeless, so that they don't feel cold outside anymore.
Please give food to those who are hungry and thirsty, so that they can have more energy to continue their lives.
Please give clothes to those who are naked, so that they can keep their dignity.
Please give them a job, so that they can find a purpose and meaning in their lives.

Please show these people Your love, God.
Please take care of them.
Please don't let them lose hope in life.

Thank You, God.

Amen

Prayer For Those Who Always Hurt Others

Dear God,

Today I wanted to pray for those who always hurt others, physically and emotionally.
It is always hard to understand why they are doing what they are doing.
They probably have a lot of wounds in the past.
But then, innocent people ended up becoming victims because of them.

God, please stop these people from doing bad things.
Please don't let them continue to cause suffering to other people.
Please make them realize that what they do is terrible.
Please heal their wounds, if any.
And please forgive them.

For the victims, please support them, God.
Please heal them and ease their pain.
It may not be fair for them, but I hope You can strengthen them.

Please be a new hope for them.

Let Your peace spread throughout the world.
Let us love each other instead of hurting each
other.

Thank You, God.

Amen

Prayer For Positivity, Joyfulness, and A Pure Heart

Dear God,

I have a favor to ask You.
I would like to become a more positive person,
more joyful, and to have a pure heart.

Instead of being negative, complaining, and
ungrateful;
please remind me to be positive.
I want to always see the best in each person and
each situation, being optimistic, and grateful.

Instead of ruminating unpleasant past events and
feel bitter and sad,
please remind me to see the beauty in my life
and appreciate it more.
Please fill my life with joy.
I want to always smile, fill my life with laughter,
spread the joy and happiness to the people
around me, as well as cheering them up.

Instead of saying things or doing things that are
hurtful to others,

please remind me to always be gentle and kind
towards them.
Instead of having bad thoughts, being selfish,
and doing other things that are shameful,
please purify myself, God.
I want to always be sincere, wish the best for
others, support them, and pray for them without
expecting to be reciprocated.

Wouldn't it be nice if I can live like this?
Okay, now that I have said it, I want to make it
happens.
So, please help me God.
Thank You.

Amen

Prayer For Wisdom

Dear God,

Today, my prayer is to ask for wisdom.
I realized that often in my life, I need wisdom.
Especially when interacting with people and
making life decisions.
Sometimes, what the world teaches me may
seem like a wisdom, but it is actually not.
But what You teach me, I know for sure that it is
the wisdom that I need.

The world encourages us to pursue freedom.
But I would only pursue it after I know how to
take responsibility of my freedom.
The world encourages us to stand up for
ourselves.
But I would only do it after I carefully examine
myself, whether I am right or I am just being
selfish.
The world encourages us to share our
experiences with the world.
But I would only do that if what I share adds
value to people instead of just to boast about
myself.

The world offers quick, easy, and instant
solution towards a problem.
But I would want to be persistent in solving the
problem without giving up.
I realize that sometimes, taking the harder and
longer route will make us grow.
The world always suggests new things that come
with bad consequences that we don't realize.
That's why I need Your guidance as I have only
limited understanding about this world.

So, please always share Your wisdom with me.
Thank You, God.

Amen

Prayer For Loving Myself

Dear God,

Today, my prayer is to love myself.
When you created me, I know that You created something good.
You equipped me with good qualities and strengths that enable me to fill this world with goodness.

When I feel like I failed to be the person I wanted to be;
Please remind me of times when I became a much better person than I expected.

When my weaknesses make me disappointed in myself;
Please remind me of my strengths that make me satisfied and confident in myself.

When my past wounds make me unable to love or to receive love fully;
Please remind me of the moments when I was able to love unconditionally;
and the lovely moments I shared with the people around me.

God, I know that I am good enough in Your
eyes, even with my imperfections.
I know that I don't have to be perfect to be loved
by You.
I want to always love my imperfect self too.
And I will always focus on being the best
version of myself.

Thank You, God, for my appearance, my talents,
my characteristics, my experiences, and my
values.
If I could be born again, I would still choose to
be myself.

Thank You God, for creating me the way I am
and loving me the way I am.

Amen

Prayer For Loving Others

Dear God,

Today, I want to pray so that I can love others sincerely.
I want to always share the love and joy with others.
I want to be a person who brings peace and who makes others feel comfortable.
I want to be a person who can always appreciate the good in others.
I want to be a person who is tolerant and forgiving towards others.
I want to become a person who can give without expecting anything back.
I want to be like You, God, who always love us unconditionally.

Sometimes, loving others means that we have to make sacrifices.
It could be sacrifices of our feelings, emotions, time, energy, money, etc.
When I don't know when to draw a line, please guide me, God.

I want to live in peace, unity, and harmony with
everybody.
Everywhere I go.
Thank You, God.

Amen

Prayer For My Relationship With You, God

Dear God,

I am very grateful to have You in my life.
The more I talk to You through prayer, the closer
I feel towards You.
I may not always hear Your answers right away,
but eventually, I always realize how real Your
presence and involvements are in my life.

From the little things that happened in my life
that seemed insignificant;
or for the things that happened that I did not
understand in the beginning;
I realize that Your plans for me are always
perfect.
You have taught me a lot of things that pushed
me to be a better person.
You are always there for me when I need hope.
You always lead me to the right direction.
You never give up on me.

It is easy to think that everything that happened
in my life was just a coincidence.

But no. If they were all coincidences, the
outcome would either be good, bad, or neutral.
But when I surrender my life to You, the
outcome is always good.
Even better than I expected.
The more I look for You, the more real Your
presence in my life is.
With You, I lack nothing and I do not need to
worry anymore.

God, I am sorry if sometimes I disappoint You.
I am sorry if I am not always loyal.
I am sorry if I sometimes prioritize other things
over You.
I am sorry if I am too busy maintaining my ego
and pride.
I am sorry if I am asking too much.
I am sorry if sometimes I am doubting You.
I hope You will never give up on me.

God, please be with me always
You are my only hope.
Thank You for everything that You have done to
me.

Amen

www.ingramcontent.com/pod-product-compliance
Lightning Source LLC
LaVergne TN
LVHW010927200726
843509LV00013B/2106